Table of Contents

Going for the Gold

Smack! Wham! Bam! It's ice hockey and curling at the Olympics. Both of these winter team sports on the ice rink are fan favorites. Hockey has been in the winter Olympics for about 100 years. Curling is newer to the Olympics, but it's a much older game. These sports get a chance to shine every four years. The best teams play their hearts out for a gold medal.

A Canadian hockey player shoots the puck in the 2014 gold medal game.

The United States and Canada played for the 1924 Olympic gold medal.

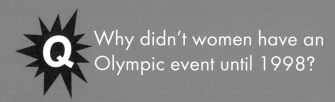 Why didn't women have an Olympic event until 1998?

Ice Hockey

The game of ice hockey is old. It has been around for about 150 years. It got its start in Canada. Soon, people around the world were playing it. Men's hockey was part of the 1920 Summer Games. The first Winter Games in 1924 also featured men's hockey. Women were playing hockey then, too. But women didn't have an Olympic event until the games in 1998.

Some people didn't think women should play such a rough sport. But women fought for the right to play.

Each hockey team has six players on the ice. One player is the **goalie**. The goalie tries to keep the puck out of the goal. Two players are **defenders**. They also help protect the goal. The right and left **wings** shoot goals. They score points for their team. The **center** helps the wings and the defenders.

The goalie is ready to block the puck.

8

The Canadian women's hockey
team huddles before a game.

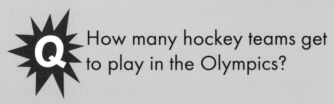

How many hockey teams get
to play in the Olympics?

Only the best teams play at the Olympics. Most are chosen for their high **rankings**. Teams are ranked based on how well they played at the last four world hockey championships. The teams with the top rankings automatically get a spot in the Olympics. The host country also gets to have a team. The rest of the teams have to face off for a chance to play.

There are spots for twelve men's teams and eight women's teams.

Great Moments

Whack! A hockey player passes the puck. Swish! Her teammate shoots. Goal! One of the most exciting women's games was also the first gold medal game. In 1998, the United States faced Canada for gold. The Canadians played hard. But the Americans kept the lead. The final score was 3–1. The US team won the first women's hockey gold medal!

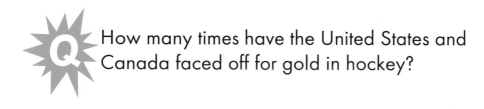 How many times have the United States and Canada faced off for gold in hockey?

The US women's team defends the goal in the 1998 gold medal game.

 The women's teams have met four times. The men's teams have met six times. Both US teams have won the gold just once in those games.

The US team celebrates winning against the Soviets in 1980.

One of the most exciting men's hockey games happened in 1980. It pitted the US against the Soviet Union. The Soviets had won gold at the last four Olympics. No one thought the Americans had a chance. But the US team pulled out all the stops. They beat the Soviets! Then they went on to bring home the gold medal. Today that game is known as "The Miracle on Ice."

Curling

Roar! A large, smooth stone rumbles down the ice. Smack! It hits another stone. This is curling. People have been playing this game for at least 500 years. It was even in the first Winter Olympics, but teams played for fun, not for medals. The game became more popular over time. Finally, it became a true Olympic sport in 1998.

 Do curling players wear ice skates?

Curling fans fill the arena at the 2010 Winter Games.

 No. They wear shoes. The shoes have sliders on them.

Canadian curlers work to guide their stone to scoring position.

Curling pits two teams against each other. Each team has four players. They play on a rectangular sheet of ice. Both teams play from the same end of the ice. The players take turns sliding their stones toward a target, called the **house**. They are aiming for the middle, or the **button**.

When a stone goes sliding down the ice, other teammates help out with **brooms**. Brooms have a soft cloth on the bottom. The sweepers use them to rub the ice in front of the moving stone. The rubbing heats up the ice just a little to melt the ice. Then the stone glides a little farther. The **skip** yells commands to the sweepers. He tells them when and how to sweep.

The German skip shouts commands to his sweepers.

So far, the red team has one point. Can the yellow team knock the red stone out?

 **Q** How many curling teams play in the Olympics?

The stones closest to the button win a point. But teams don't just try to win points. They try to take points away from the other team. How? They use their stones to knock the other team's stones out of the house. Wham! Red knocks out yellow! At the end of the game, the team with the most points wins.

 There are spots for 10 men's teams and 10 women's teams. The teams with the top rankings get eight of the spots. The other teams compete for the last two spots.

Curling Greats

Curling was invented in Great Britain, but Canada has the teams with the most medals. Even so, the men's team from Great Britain is one to watch. In 2014, they ended up in the gold medal game against Canada. Great Britain played hard, but lost the game. This silver medal was their first medal since 1924.

 Has the United States ever won gold?

British curlers throw for a chance at the gold medal in 2014.

 No. The men's team won the bronze in 2006. This is the only curling medal that either US team has won.

A mixed doubles team competes at the Youth Olympic Games in 2016.

Curling might look like a dull game. But people can't get enough of the roaring stones, the amazing takeout shots, and the fast sweeping. The Olympics has even added a new curling event. It's called mixed doubles. Each team has one man and one woman. Mixed doubles will be part of the 2018 Olympics. Eight teams will compete.

Bring on the Olympics!

Wham! Bam! Roar! Smack! The Olympics is an exciting time. You can see hockey and curling at their best. Players go head to head. They shoot goals or aim for the house. Who will bring home the gold? Tune in to the Olympics to find out!

Canadian hockey players celebrate winning the gold medal at the 2014 Winter Games.

29

Glossary

broom The tool curlers use to melt the ice to help control where the stone goes.

button The middle of the target, or house, in curling.

center In hockey, usually the strongest, fastest player who can either score goals or help defend.

defender Hockey players that work to stop the other team from scoring.

goalie The hockey player that guards the goal and blocks shots.

house In curling, the target players aim for. A curling rink has two targets, one at each end.

ranking A team's position compared to other teams; the best team in the world has the highest ranking.

skip The leader of a curling team that tells the sweepers when and how to sweep.

wing Hockey players who work to score goals.

Read More

Johnson, Robin. *Ice Hockey and Curling*. New York: Crabtree Publishing Co., 2010.

Kwak, Sarah. *Face Off! Top 10 Lists of Everything in Hockey*. New York: Time Inc. Books, 2015.

Thorp, Claire. *Curling*. Chicago: Heinemann–Raintree, 2014.

Websites

International Ice Hockey Federation
www.iihf.com/home-of-hockey/championships/olympics

Time for Kids: Winter Olympic Events
http://www.timeforkids.com/news/winter-olympic-events/137746

World Curling Federation
www.worldcurling.org/pyeongchang-2018-olympic-winter-games

Index

About the Author

Laura Hamilton Waxman has written and edited many nonfiction books for children. She loves learning about new things—like ice hockey and curling—and sharing what she's learned with her readers. She lives in St. Paul, Minnesota.